To the Dentist

Written by Caleb Burroughs
Illustrated by C.A. Nobens
Cover illustrated by Louise Gardner

Louis Weber, C.E.O., Publications International, Ltd.
7373 North Cicero Avenue, Lincolnwood, Illinois 60712

Ground Floor, 59 Gloucester Place, London W1U 8JJ

Customer Service: 1-800-595-8484 or customer_service@pilbooks.com

www.pilbooks.com

Permission is never granted for commercial purposes.

p i kids is a registered trademark of Publications International, Ltd.

ISBN-13: 978-1-4127-9183-0
ISBN-10: 1-4127-9183-9

8 7 6 5 4 3 2 1

publications international, ltd.

Hi! My name is Pedro. Today my mommy took me to the dentist for a checkup. A checkup is when the dentist checks to see how your teeth are doing.

We got to the dentist's office and sat in the waiting room. There were lots of fun toys and books! Soon I heard the dentist call my name.

"Hello, Pedro," the dentist said with a big, friendly smile. "How are you doing?"

The first thing I did was show her my tooth that was loose. I had just noticed it that morning.

"There is nothing to worry about, Pedro," she said. "A loose tooth means that you are growing."

"It does?" I asked.

"Your baby teeth will loosen and fall out," the dentist said.

"They fall out?" I asked.

"It's okay," the dentist said. "Your permanent teeth will grow back in their place. Those are the teeth you'll have forever."

With a wink, she said, "Once a tooth falls out, put it under your pillow. Then the tooth fairy will bring you a surprise!"

Next, the dentist took special pictures called X-rays. The X-rays showed the inside of my mouth. I could see what my teeth looked like!

"Your teeth look healthy, Pedro," the dentist said. "You must take good care of them."

I told the dentist that I always brush and that's why my teeth look so white and healthy.

Root

Crown

Gums

Canine

I thought the X-rays were cool. But not as cool as the things on the dentist's table.

"What are these?" I asked.

"Those are the tools I use to clean and examine my patients' teeth. First is a sprayer. The next tool is a suction, which is a vacuum cleaner for your mouth. Then we have a scraper, a mirror, and a tongue depressor."

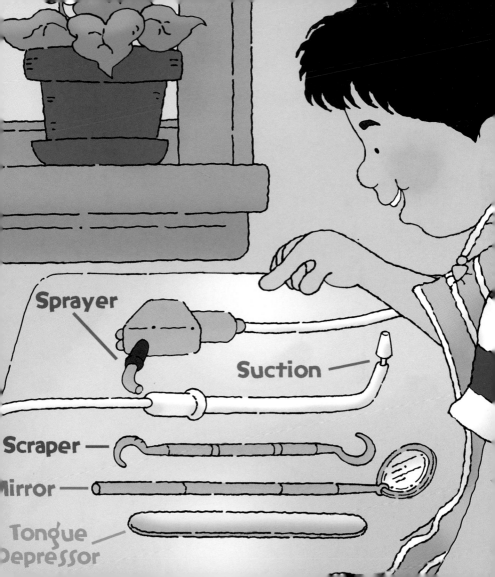

Sprayer

Suction

Scraper

Mirror

Tongue Depressor

The dentist had me sit down in a big, comfy chair.

"Open your mouth and say 'Ahhh,' please," she said.

"Ahhh," I said.

She looked inside my mouth with the special mirror tool. Using the mirror, she could see every part of every tooth.

"Your teeth look great!" she told me.

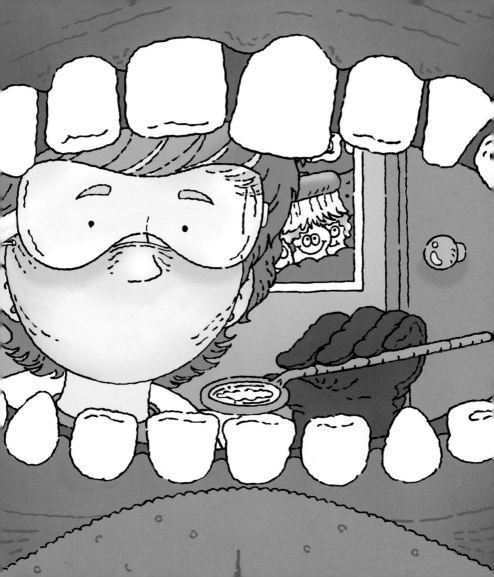

After the dentist cleaned my teeth with the scraper tool, she helped me out of the chair.

"That sprayer you used tickled my tongue!" I told her.

Then she reminded me how important it is to take good care of my teeth.

"Brush and floss every day," she said. "And try to eat healthy foods instead of sweets."

My mommy was so proud
of me. And so was the dentist.
She gave me a new toothbrush.
I'll make sure to use it so I'll
have a good checkup the next
time I visit her!